Fierce Autistic Heart

Michelle Swan

Books in the "Living Autistically" series:

Fierce Autistic Heart	(2024)
Authentic Autistic Living	(2024)
Perfectly Normal Autistic	(2024)

Original cover art by Emory Thorsen.

ISBN 978-0-6488711-4-9 (print - paperback)
ISBN 978-0-6488711-7-0 (EPUB)
ISBN 978-0-9756585-0-5 (PDF)

Published in Australia by Michelle Swan
© Michelle Swan 2024
This work is copyright. Apart from any use permitted under the Copyright Act 1968, no part may be reproduced by any process, nor may any other exclusive right be exercised, without the permission of the author.
contact@hellomichelleswan.com

This book is for informational purposes only. It does not constitute advice, and should not be used as replacement for professional support and/or diagnosis.

This book is dedicated to
the six spectacularly quirky individuals
to whom I am a parent,
who have so far survived me figuring out the
important things about life, myself and parenting
along the way,
and who have been my greatest teachers.

contents

introduction	i
recognising	1
becoming	8
rearranging	12
angry	15
criticised	22
defined	28
diagnosed	34
growing	39
love	42
wings	44
pathways	47
human	51
mind	54
body	57
heart	61
fierce	65

introduction

We get such mixed messages from all around us about how we are supposed to feel about ourselves, don't we? One advertisement says we are "worth it", another says we are "the most important person in the world", yet another tells us to care for ourselves first because no one else will. But somewhere else we are told to be humble, and put others first. Pride is seen as something we should hide, and shame is pushed on us from all directions. Eat less, exercise more, put this on your face, dress this way to hide your flaws, and don't behave in ways that others will find weird.

I spent a lot of time trying to conform to all of those messages, even the ones that conflicted with each other. These days I know I am weird, and

I am quite comfortable with that. I know the ways in which I am different from many other people. I know what I need to do in order to live well and meet my own needs. And I am quite proud that I have reached a stage in my life where I can honestly say I happy to be me, in the body I have, with my own unique brain, and with the strengths and challenges that come with it.

I wasn't always proud of myself. In fact, I haven't always liked myself. Before I knew I was Autistic I mostly found myself confusing. The process to understanding myself has been a long one, that started many years ago. It took me 6 years of reading, asking questions, self reflection, and personal growth. It's been 8 years since I "came out" publicly as Autistic. Understanding yourself better is always a good thing, I think. Recognising myself as Autistic is the most powerful thing that I've ever experienced. Looking back over my life with a fresh lens has been a gift. Learning to look after myself in ways that truly work for me has been life changing.... Possibly life saving.

In this book, a collection of short essays, I'm going to try to tell you what that process was like for me, and how I have learned to like my Autistic identity. It's my unique story, but I've been told by so many other Autistic people that when they read my words they feel seen and heard, so I know that my story is at least somewhat representative of the experience of others in the Autistic community. It's just a short book, because lots of people find big books overwhelming, especially when they are in a period of time during which life is hard. Each chapter addresses a concept or a key point I have focussed on as I've moved toward a positive Autistic self identity. Whether you are reading with a desire to understand yourself better, or a loved one more, I hope these chapters are useful to you.

Michelle

recognising

{first published in December 2015}

Sometimes things change quickly, and it is easy to see the change. Sometimes they shift ever so slowly, and the change kind of sneaks itself in without you realising it is there, until suddenly you turn around and everything is different. Growing up can be a bit like that. And as I get older, I am learning you never stop growing up, and identity is a dynamic thing.

Growing up, I was parented so that life was structured in ways that, unknown to both my parents and I at the time, simultaneously suited me well and taught me to be compliant and chameleon like. Even though inside I usually felt I was never quite right enough and not quite good enough, on the outside, by using a combination of mimicry and invisibility, I got by.

Friendships involved attaching myself to one or two people I cherished and staying within that safe circle. Getting through high school involved many hours hard work behind the scenes that I denied enduring to justify my less than spectacular results.

When things went wrong I endured the knowledge that I was wrongly accused in silence, both because it was easier than the confrontation involved in defending myself (mostly because the beautiful strings of words flying through my head explaining what had actually happened got stuck there and never made it out my mouth), and because I honestly believed (and am still learning to unbelieve) that my role in life is to make other people happy no matter the cost to me.

Making other people happy became my thing. If everyone around me was happy, I was content because there was no conflict. I hid my needs deep inside and moved through life on the constant brink of shutdown.

I was not happy. I did not believe I was unhappy, but I knew I was uncomfortable.

I remember my mother telling me once, as I lamented being chronically and unhealthily underweight, that when I became happy with my life I would put on weight. About 10 years ago, that began to happen.

It didn't start with a feeling of happiness. It started with a feeling of giving up. I gave up trying so hard. I was too tired. I knew I was not enough to do all the things I had been doing. I was at the end of my coping. I began to let go.

Since then, there has been a slow process of realising I am me. Which may sound odd, but it is what happened. I stopped doing and pretending to myself, and began to recognise myself.

I am not a naturally tidy person. I do not naturally have good organisational skills. I do not thrive when I expect myself to be around people a lot. I do not like unexpected change at all- it makes me ill. Realising the 'do nots' helped me find the 'I likes'.

I like writing to express my thoughts. I like to be home a lot. I like having friends, but just a couple of good friends who I can really engage with. I am passionate about justice and equality. I am prepared to stand up with those who need help standing up to be heard, and I can do that well when I acknowledge my needs within that context.

The process actually began when my family members were diagnosed with their own disabilities. The first step in recognising myself was learning to look after myself well, so I could be healthy and available to support them. Part of that was finding community who understood my families needs. For me this was the Autistic community.

Over time I learned, with the support of new friends, the word neurodivergent. That was a revelation. I saw myself in it immediately, but took my time in claiming it as part of my identity because change is hard even when it is good.

I thought it, then began to speak it, until it was part of the fabric of me. It was like being given a gift, and as I allowed myself to identify as neurodivergent, and therefore to notice what my tolerances and limits are, the more I have grown to know that these things have been needs for my whole life that up until now I have managed to take care of alone without inconveniencing anyone else, but that the cost to me has been huge emotionally, physically and mentally.

I began to identify as "Neurodivergent NOS ", believing I would not ever find a specific label. It was a play on medical diagnostic language using "not otherwise specified" and it suited me well for a time.

As I talked through some of this with my autistic friends, I grew increasingly aware of how similar my life experiences have been to theirs. Their openness and willingness to share with me helped me to gain confidence to stop using my children's needs as cover to have my own needs met.

I needed to allow myself to be me, or the slow slide to burnout I had been feeling would become a quick fall.

At the same time as I was deciding on the need to stop and allow myself to be me, four autistic people (including my own child) all asked me in various ways why I do not think I am Autistic. The idea was not new to me- I had even talked to my psychologist to explore the idea over a year before, but, as often happens when women get through 40 years of life before questioning their assumed neurology, she kind of said 'nah- too high functioning', and so I moved on. My answer to my friends was that I have been coming to that conclusion over the past couple of years, but had not been confident to say so.

One dear friend edged me closer to confidence ever so aptly when they questioned "are you feeling less NOS?". I cried that night after telling that friend, "Identifying as neurodivergent, I gave myself permission not to pass. Now the less I pass the more autistic I feel." and having them respond "Oh yeah I GET THAT SO HARD….".

I was so relieved I barely slept the night that I shared with another friend how hard I was finding it to hold everything together and they responded, "I think we all feel like that. You know what though, once we identify as autistic, it's pretty common for all the things we were doing to keep it all together to sort of come crumbling down for a bit. We realise how much effort the whole thing took."

Having affirmation from them was so helpful, and has allowed me to begin seeing things through a specific lens that answers many more questions than it creates for me.

I think I am autistic. I have been thinking it for a long while now. I am ready to speak it, until it becomes part of the fabric of me.

becoming

{first published in December 2015}

So here I am, becoming Autistic. Not literally, of course. I have been Autistic my whole life. But I am figuratively becoming Autistic as I learn to recognise in myself the things I do to move through the life I want.

I am becoming Autistic as I own how much I find it hard to be touched by people I don't know very well, and how noises bother me, and how I use screen time to disengage, how much I can't do multiple phone calls in a day, how much I love my solitude.

I am becoming Autistic as I grow more confident to claim my identity as a person whose needs are not the same as the majority, but who has found community with others like myself.

I am becoming Autistic as I recognise myself, allow myself to just be, become comfortable in my own

skin, and learn to care for myself in the best ways for me- not only after everyone else seems to be happy I have met their expectations of what I should be.
I am becoming Autistic and it is good.

It comes with tiredness though. It feels a little like changing the rules. It takes so much thinking about to see myself differently than what I've been told, and have told myself.

It comes with uncertainty. What if this feeling of relating to Autistic people is that for the first time ever I feel really accepted by a group of people I respect and enjoy knowing, and what if I am making it up? I find myself thinking," well, if I have come this far.... why now do I think this? am I being a chameleon now, or is this truly discovery?"

In the past my reason for thinking I'm not Autistic was that I didn't perceive myself to be disabled enough. But deep down I know I just was passing to myself. And then I recognise myself again. And I relax, because it doesn't matter what others think, this journey is mine.

It comes with growing confidence. I am not prepared to go through the process of pathologising myself for the sake of formalities. I spent my life feeling not good enough and like my role was to please others. It is only the identification with the term neurodivergent that has begun to free me from that, and I will not force myself back there for a piece of paper.

It comes with a fair bit of fear too. It is hard knowing what some people's reactions will be- I have been in advocacy long enough to know how many people treat those who are openly Autistic- and choosing to experience that. And there is fear that I will not be believed or seen as credible because I do not have a life that looks to others like it backs it up. I feel like everyone has seen me being a fraud by passing as neurotypical, and now if I say I am Autistic they will call that the fraudulent thing. It's hard to put into words. It's like realising there is an easier way to be, but knowing many non autistic people think being autistic is worse, so they won't understand why I'd want to be that way.

It comes with increasing boldness, when I am in the middle of fear and worry, and I discover strong words that encourage me to be myself and live in ways that work for me. I remember my passion for justice and my desire to walk before my children and model to them what it means to be proud and determined and unapologetically oneself.

So, I am becoming Autistic, and it is liberating.

rearranging

{first published in December 2015}

Shaping an expanded identity gives opportunities not many other situations give. Looking back over my life through a different lens adds perspective and dimension to my experience. It explains and validates.

It helps me to accept myself and changes my internal dialogue.
I am replacing "you should be able to do these simple things without needing to have a day off afterward" and the frustrated internal cries of "why do you find this so hard? what is wrong with you?" with "it is alright to plan to do just one thing today so I have energy for more tomorrow".

I am unlearning "my highest priority is to make sure everyone else's needs and wants are met first" and affirming "it is important to make sure I look after myself".

I am losing the feeling of "I don't fit anywhere, I am always just on the outside" and finding a community of friends who understand me and are supporting me to have confidence to say "this is me, take me as I am".

It is an opportunity for self reflection and reprioritising.
It is a chance to look at what I love about myself and foster it.
It is the freedom to acknowledge where I struggle and ask for help.
It is a raw process. It is taking this part from here and looking at it in detail, deciding if it helps or hurts, then grafting it where it belongs. It feels more comfortable over all to have things in their new places, but the edges sting where they were pulled at, and sometimes there is an empty space left where it was that I am not sure what to fill with yet.

It is a tentative process. At this stage uncomfortably influenced by my worry that others will not like this me that they perceive is new, and different and changing.

It is an exciting process. As I pull at the parts of myself that have always felt a bit out of place and move them to where they feel better, I discover who I really am, and see the potential of who I can be.

It is a hopeful process. I feel hope that I will find an internal integrity I have so far found elusive. I feel hopeful because I see that I am uncovering strengths and challenges that once acknowledged are leading me to paths I can tread with confidence and pride.
It is growing into myself, rearranging myself a bit at a time, building authenticity until I am happy with what I see. Then showing my emerging Autistic self to others without shame.

angry

{first published in 2017}

I know we can't change the past. I know that things in our past help us become who we are, and that is often a really positive thing. I know hindsight gives clarity and we probably shouldn't spend too much time looking back with regret. But I have to admit I'm feeling angry about something that has happened, and happens to lots of people, that has meant I missed out on something really good for a long time. Looking back could be dangerous if we dwell there and don't move on, but if we are willing I think there is something to be learned from it.

It was 10 years ago I was in a psychologists office when she said to me, "I know your focus coming here is to get your son the help and support he needs, and that his autism diagnosis is a bit overwhelming. But it is a good thing, and one day we should make time to talk about you." I looked at her confused. She smiled kindly. There was a pause, and I moved the conversation back to my son.

About 6 months later we moved an hour and a half drive away and I changed psychologists. I just remembered recently that this conversation had happened.

I didn't remember it when the next child was identified as autistic. I didn't remember it when I was struggling to balance overwhelm and what I thought was depression with parenting 6 kids. I didn't even remember it 5 years ago year when I asked the psychologist I was seeing then if she thought I could be autistic.

I remembered it when I was writing "becoming autistic". I didn't document it then because I was slightly unsure I was remembering correctly. I mean, how could I have forgotten that? It should have been really significant, and I forgot it. I've been thinking about that a fair bit the past week, and I do want to document it, because I think I know why I forgot.

I forgot that my psychologist had said she thought I might be autistic because I dismissed the thought almost as soon as I left her office. Why? Because I believed it wasn't possible.

I was not disabled. I was uncomfortable with the thought that the word disabled could be applied to me. I had not needed support to get through school. I was studying at uni for a second degree. I was married. I had (at that stage) 5 children. I didn't have language problems. I wasn't like "them", the other autistic people I knew of. I had bought into the stereotypes and stigma around autism, albeit subconsciously, so that I honestly believed that could not be me.

The idea of myself as autistic was so foreign that rather than confront it I got busy ignoring the evidence. I ignored the fact that I dropped out of a subject of study at uni because the exam was going to be held in a place I had never been to and I couldn't cope with getting myself there. I ignored the fact that I frequently had days when I was so overwhelmed that I spent the day in bed, then got up just before my husband got home from work, did a quick tidy and pretended I was fine. I ignored the fact that I had already started to use my son's needs as an excuse to not do things that I didn't want to do. I ignored the anxiety underlying everything I did while trying to be what

I thought other people wanted me to be. I let the lure of indistinguishability, and the pull of external expectations run my life. I ignored the fact that when I disagreed with something I routinely didn't say anything about it because the thought of a conflict robbed me of my ability to articulate the words formed inside my head. And I missed out on an opportunity.

It would be another 3 years before I started to meet other autistic adults and begin to learn that autism in adults looks different than autism in children. It's logical, so you'd think I'd have realised before, but I didn't.

It took another year before I realised that autistic adult women are actually a lot like me!

It took another year before I was brave enough to ask about it in a therapy session. I was told "too high functioning", so I put it aside.

It was 6 more months and many gentle prompts from caring friends before I was comfortable talking about it with them.

And here I am. 10 years after first being offered the opportunity to know myself better and allow myself to move into this liberating stage of self acceptance.

Why do I feel angry? Well, it's because I lost time. It's because I could have been learning all this great stuff about living well as myself years ago. It's because it has taken so long for me be able to let go of the false ideas I had about autistic people. It's because the ableism and untruths taught to me by society had me locked up in denial for so long and if I hadn't been locked up my children would have benefitted. It's because I am not the only one.

I feel angry that we are so caught up in the falsehood of "normal" being better, that people don't feel confident to express themselves honestly. I feel angry that diversity is feared, instead of acknowledged as valuable as necessary. I feel angry to know that people were fighting to change these things long before that first suggestion was made to me, and I didn't even know. I feel angry that people are still fighting and so many people still don't know. I feel angry that many who do see neurodivergent people stand up for themselves will do all they can to get them to sit down and be quiet. I feel angry that so much of the public discussion about autism is conducted by people who are not autistic- people who say they want to help, but who won't let us speak for ourselves to say what would actually be helpful.

I feel angry that, because our society devalues and silences diversity, I missed out on knowing myself. I feel angry that I contributed to my own silencing for a time. I feel angry that so many people are still in the position I was, and it's really not their fault- they just haven't been able to receive the message yet because it is really really hard to, when all the other messages are so incredibly loud.

I want you to know, if you are wondering about neurodivergence, if someone is suggesting, if you are just not sure- keep looking, keep exploring, keep asking. Don't dismiss it in favour
of accepting the stereotypes. Don't let the stigma put you off. Don't let misunderstanding, outright denial, or fear of the truth, stop you from recognising yourself. Knowing yourself is more important. Understanding who you are is worth it. Being angry about the tyranny of expectation of normality is justified and right.

It has been hard to confront all these thoughts and memories from my past. But it is worth it. I, and my right to live my life well, are worth it. You, and your right to live your life well, are worth it.

criticised

When I was in primary school, I went to stay with my grandparents one night that I have not forgotten, even 40 or so years later. A while ago I received a message on my blog that I doubt I will ever forget. The two events are separated by decades, but remembering the first just after the occurrence of the second started a chain of thoughts that brought me to a place of realisation I was not expecting.

The reason I haven't forgotten the sleep over at my grandparents is because my grandmother called me a liar. At the time I was confused and angry and hurt. Time heals, and I am no longer upset by this memory. I can now see it from her perspective and I understand why. The evidence supported her belief, and I did not say anything to her to give her information to the contrary. In fact I didn't say anything to her at all.

I had been asked to have a shower, which I did, but at that point in my life I preferred a bath and as her shower had a deep base I blocked up the drain with my wash cloth and sat in the bottom of the shower cubicle. Because I had not stood up there was no water spray around the shower screen. Because I had played around at cleaning after I turned off the water there had been no obvious wetness in the bottom of the shower either. It was fair that she thought I had not showered, and she confronted me about it. I said nothing in response to her question "Why did you not have a shower?". I thought, "I did have a shower". But I didn't say it. She asked, "Did you have a shower?" and I nodded. She questioned me further, but I remained silent, which she took as an admission of my guilt, and I was sent to bed crying and feeling disgraced.

I can remember numerous times as a child when I was unable to speak on finding myself in a conflict situation, or confronted over my behaviour by someone in authority. I had strings of perfectly acceptable words formed in my head, I could read them from across my forehead over and over, but I could not make myself speak them. It is known as situational mutism, and is fairly common in Autistic people. Of course I didn't know that as a child.

This still happens to me as an adult, and it is frustrating now. Then it was overwhelming and distressing, especially as I would often just cry in front of my accuser, red-faced and full of shame and embarrassment, and hurry to retreat somewhere that I could safely shut down for a while.

A while back, an anonymous person left a comment on my website, telling me that Autistic people can't fulfil their potential or be productive members of society, are a burden that suck up tax dollars by claiming welfare, that parents should be able to know the probability of having an Autistic child so they can choose if they want to risk being burdened, and that Autism should be eradicated.

This comment made me angry, but I felt no shame. It was a venomous attack on me and my family and friends, but I did not feel disgraced. The person wrote it intending to upset me with their hateful opinion of me, but I felt no embarrassment. I know that this persons opinion is not uncommon, but I was not overwhelmed or distressed. It shook me up a bit, certainly, but even though I had a few moments of questioning myself it did not leave me in a state of shut down.

You see, as a child I did not know why I experienced difficulty with communication when stressed. I do now. I have learned so much about myself, and that has lead to being able to accept myself and be proud of who I am. I do not need to be part of the neuromajority to know I have value. I do not need to conform to standards of typicality to have something of worth to offer. I can be disabled and still have a right to life without being told autism should be eradicated. I can need support sometimes without being considered a burden, and I can still support others even if I don't do it by paying as much tax as they do.

The shame and embarrassment that surfaced often in my childhood and young adult years came from not knowing who I was, assuming I was someone I was not, and as a result, trying to be someone I couldn't.

I see people throwing around the word "Autistic" as an insult. Claiming "Autistic" is a label that they don't want for their child. Accusing us of using "Autistic" as an excuse to be lazy and dependent. Saying "Autistic" means ill, diseased and broken.

To me "Autistic" means identity. It is a label I am proud to share with my children and my friends. It is a reason that explains so much. It is word that describes a way of being, and a gift that gave me permission to just be myself.

None of that is new to me. These are thoughts I am comfortable with and have written about before. But processing these two events over the past week has brought me to a conclusion that surprised me a little: **I am comfortable being criticised for being Autistic.**

As I was thinking about writing this chapter, I drafted "I'd rather be criticised for things that are true about me than for incorrect assumptions others have made about me", but then I realised that is wrong on a couple of levels. Firstly, I'd rather not be criticised at all for simply being myself and because myself is not what people expected. Secondly, even though I tell people I am Autistic that doesn't mean they won't make incorrect assumptions about me.

So instead I will say,
I know that, as part of a neurominority group, criticism of the person I am and the way I live in order to be my best self is inevitable. It is illogical

and narrow minded, but it will happen because our society does not value difference or diversity. I am comfortable with that, because it is still easier to tell people the truth about myself. I would rather be able to respond to criticisms with facts that will hopefully increase others understanding of who I am, and maybe help shift their ideas about Autism a little, than to be constantly defending myself from within the context of an assumption that I am something I am not.

As a child I had neither the insight nor the tools to advocate for myself, but I do now. I am older, understand who I am, am more capable of self-advocacy, and I have the strength that comes from knowing there is a community behind me who understands, accepts and likes me as I am. A community that will stand with me in saying, "You can go ahead and criticise all you like, but we are here and we have every right to be, so your words will not stop us from living our lives and living them well."

defined

When we meet someone new, it is expected that we get to know each other to some extent. The context of the meeting tends to dictate the sorts of questions that are typically part of the conversation. Where are you from? What do you do? Do you have any children? There are also some answers that are typically considered to be appropriate, and some answers that will generally attract a negative reaction.

I think what we are trying to do when we engage in these discussions is to find out the other persons identity. Who are they? What defines them? Do I have anything in common with them? I guess this is not an inherently bad thing, but it is problematic when you consider the fact that we tend to make certain assumptions about a person based on their answers that, if we are honest with ourselves, are often assumptions made in error.

Let me introduce myself:

I am Michelle.
I am a woman.
I am a mother.
(*I wonder: did you assume anything so far? Maybe about the way I look? How old I am? How many children I have?*)
I have two University degrees.
I have been in community building and advocacy roles for around 10 years now.
I am founder and a Director of a not for profit community organisation.
I run my own small business providing support to neurodivergent people in my local community.
(*I wonder what you think I studied? I wonder if you have assumed anything about my income? Or what my days look like, and how much time I spend working? Have you formed an idea about how successful or how capable I am? I wonder if you think I am like you or not?*)

I could go on, but I think you see what I mean by assumptions. The things I have just disclosed to you would be considered positive things. I can change your perception of them by adding more specific information if I want to. Your values and experience will influence how that perception changes. For example, when I say I have six children, you might want to ask "all with the same guy?" (yes, that happens), or you may comment "do you really think that is responsible?" (that happens too), you might exclaim "you must be mad!" (happened once), or you might smile wistfully and say "you are so lucky" (which has also happened).

Your values and experience will also influence how you react when I say "I am Autistic". My experience tells me that there are a large number of people who will think quite differently of me when I say that.

Some of them will think how inspirational it is that I can be Autistic and do all these other things. Some people will assume that I am less capable than I am. Some won't know how to process the information because looking at me and trying to reconcile my life with their ideas about autism creates an incongruence for them.

Some people will default to trying to correct my language, insisting I am "a person with autism" because "autism doesn't define you". But it does.

Autism does define me, and it was a relief to be able to settle into that definition because it answered questions and empowered me to be able to live my life the way that works best for me.

I know that some people think that being Autistic is not a positive thing, that autism causes difficulties and struggles for both Autistic people and their families. I will not deny that being Autistic can be hard sometimes. But I see that as a problem society causes, not a problem that being Autistic causes. Much in the same way as a woman advancing a career is disadvantaged by discrepancies in pay scales and access to maternity and parental leave, it is difficult being Autistic when society is so determined to see Autistic people as burdens who need "special" help that is often viewed as being too difficult to provide.

So, let me re-introduce myself, in more detail, so we can move past some assumptions.

I am Michelle.
I am a woman, who doesn't place much value in society's ideas about typical gender roles.
I have 6 children.
Our family is wonderfully neurodiverse and neurodivergent, and we do everything we can to ensure we all live our lives well in ways that we

choose, working toward goals that we set for ourselves.

I have two University degrees. One in teaching and one in psychology. Earning those degrees was very difficult for me, and I am very proud of them, even though I am not a student who achieves high grades.

I have been in community building and advocacy roles for around 10 years now. I started off in a volunteer capacity in informal, community based settings, where I worked to help people find good peer support and to gain confidence in their own ability to advocate for themselves. I have a heart for mentoring, and I am good at it. I now run my own business in mentoring, advocacy and education.

I am founder and a Director of a not for profit community organisation, that exists to support neurodivergent people in finding community, support and real inclusion in their local communities.

I run my own small business, founded and now team leading a neurodiversity hub in my local community.

I am 48.

I am a late identified, proud Autistic person, who is just as happy to have Autism define me as I am any of the other characteristics I have shared with you.

Being Autistic makes me who I am, it influences how I think, what I am passionate about, and how I approach engaging with those passions. Knowing I am Autistic helps me make wise and self affirming decisions about how I live my life and care for my own needs, and is an empowering and positive part of my identity.

diagnosed

I think it's necessary to talk about diagnosis of neurodivergence. Mostly because it's not that important.

I was self identified as autistic - undiagnosed - for five years before I received an official medical diagnosis.

I was publicly self identified as autistic - undiagnosed - for five years.

I worked as an autistic mentor and advocate - undiagnosed - for five years.

I first realised I was probably autistic during a stage of my life in which paying for a diagnosis was completely impossible. Diagnoses cost money. A lot of money! I did not have a lot of money, so diagnosis was inaccessible to me.

Even when I did eventually have the money, diagnosis requires a competent and available professional to complete the diagnostic process. Where I live, those professionals are few and far between. Wait lists to see a psychologist in my local area are more than a year long, and many of the best practitioners are not accepting new clients, even onto their wait lists. I ended up seeing someone well out of my local area.

Diagnosis is difficult to get in most places in the world, especially for adults.

So, for five years I did not have one.

And I didn't need one.

In all of those five years, not a single time did I need to show proof of a diagnostic process or confirmation of my neurotype. My experiences and lifestyle spoke for themselves.

On top of not needing a diagnosis, I didn't really want one. I wasn't interested in going through a process in which I was required to talk about all the challenges I have, all the things others perceive as being wrong with me, and all the ways I have felt inadequate over the years. I was trying so hard to develop a positive sense of self, why would I counter that work by putting myself through an unnecessary diagnostic process?

I still don't *need* a diagnosis. But I did end up wanting one. I was fortunate enough to eventually have the money and a psychologist available who could help me.

There were a few reasons I ended up wanting an official diagnosis.

One of the reasons was that I was that I wanted to know what the process felt like. Not just a theoretical knowledge of the diagnostic tools that I had gained from my studies and observing my children being diagnosed. I wanted to know first hand how it felt to be asked those questions. I wanted to feel the nerves and the uncertainty. I wanted to know what it was like so that I could talk to my clients from my own first hand experience, to support them to debrief their own diagnoses with a true understanding.

Another reason I wanted a diagnosis was because I had a fear of being asked if I was diagnosed and then being berated or belittled, or treated as an imposter. This fear confused me a little, because it wasn't based on my experience, and because I was completely sure of myself and my autistic identity. But it was there nonetheless, and I knew I would feel more confident in a professional capacity if I was "officially autistic".

But mostly, I was curious. I wanted to hear from someone what areas it seemed I was having the most challenges. I wanted the extra nuance that comes with the details in a diagnostic report. I'm glad I went through with it. I ended up being surprised by some of the insights I received. I was diagnosed as having level two support needs, when I had expected to be told I have level one support needs. Apparently I find some things harder than I realised! That can happen when life on "hard mode" is your normal!!

I hope that people who are identified later in life as being autistic don't feel like they have to subject themselves to a diagnostic process in order to be able to confidently say they are autistic. Knowing yourself is way more important than a doctor giving you a piece of paper.

Diagnosis can be a gateway to accessing supports in work settings, or funding (like NDIS in Australia) if that is something that is necessary for you to have your support needs met.

But diagnosis does not change you, or make you more credible in any meaningful way.

I'm glad I have a diagnosis, but I didn't need one in order to live my life, and I know that a diagnosis is not what everyone wants.

growing

Shortly after I publicly "came out" as Autistic I was asked why I would identify as disabled or allow a label like autism to be applied to me. I didn't quite know what to say at the time, except to tell the person that labels aren't negative and that I found it helpful in understanding myself.

For a few years before, I spent a lot of time thinking and saying that I didn't think I could do things, and avoiding doing things. Before that I spent most of my time doing what was expected of me by everyone else, and suffering in silence the effects it had on me; burnout, anxiety, overwhelm, sensory overload, exhaustion, confusion, self doubt, self criticism, self punishment.

In the 12 months since I started identifying as autistic, I: began to work for pay again after almost a decade, both as a contractor and for my own small business; co-edited a book; travelled overseas for the first time in more than 2 decades; was involved in some amazing advocacy projects; became confident in practicing karate; competed in karate tournaments; lost weight; navigated some really tricky personal stuff without losing my ability to do other things in life while it was going on; continued to support my children in their varying education settings and other activities.

The year since I first publicly stated I am autistic and disabled was the most exciting and productive in a long time. Not to say that I didn't have moments of self doubt and drops in self confidence. Even now, after 10 years, I still struggle with a lot of things, just the same as before. But I'm getting more done, and enjoying my life more. I'm pretty sure all this has been made possible because I now understand myself better, I have been giving myself permission to acknowledge my needs and care for myself in ways that met those needs, and I have friends and a support network who understand me too and who offer just the right words when I need them.

I know that not everyone who realises that are neurodivergent has the same experience as I do in quickly finding life more manageable. For some people it takes a lot longer. We are all different and our lives unfold in ways that reflect those differences. I feel fortunate that this was my experience, and if it's different for you that doesn't mean you are doing something wrong.

I learned 3 important lessons in that first year, and I think these things will be helpful for anyone to think on:
1. Self understanding is an empowering thing.
2. Self advocacy, though tiring and frustrating at times, is a liberating journey.
3. The value and power of an understanding and supportive community of true peers can not be measured.

So now if someone were to ask me why I would identify as disabled or autistic when so many see that as a negative thing, I would answer, "Because when I am strong enough to acknowledge who I really am, when I am proud of my imperfect self, even in the face of criticism and discrimination; when I take steps to meet my needs, and am open with others about my need to do that and my need for them to help at times; and when I am wise enough to lean into my community for support, that is when I can live as my best self."

love

Part of the work of becoming Autistic is learning to see yourself in a new way and accepting that you are valuable and acceptable, just as you are. This was a large part of the self care I did in the first year after I realised I am Autistic. It continues to be something I actively pay attention to. It is, I suppose, self love in action.

I am drawn to the idea of love as a verb- an action that requires conscious and deliberate thought and decision making. To me love as a feeling is unreliable and changeable past the stage of establishing a relationship. Love as an action is required in order to keep a relationship alive and healthy. Love as an action involves choosing to do things for, to, and with a person for the purposes of showing them love and ensuring their needs are met in ways that they like and need. I apply this form of love to my relationships, romantic and platonic, family and friend, as much as I am able. I am learning to apply it to myself now, in practical ways, as I become increasingly aware of who I am, what I need and how I can meet my needs in positive and useful ways within the context of a busy family life and an active advocacy life. This means loving all of myself, including the parts that in the past I have spent time berating for not being "normal" or "good enough".

It sometimes strikes me as being ironic that I spend a large portion of my time advocating the right of every person to be accepted and treated fairly, regardless of disability or neurology, yet I still struggle to extend the same thinking to myself internally. It is a conscious effort to refrain from thinking of myself in ways that are judgemental and unaccepting.

I am learning to love my neurodivergent self. It is a process that requires conscious and deliberate thought and decision making. It is love as a verb. It involves positive self talk. It requires good practice of self care. It allows graciousness extended toward myself. It demands change in previously learned ways of thinking and old habits. It is extending graciousness to myself the same way I do for others. It is reminding myself that I am enough, just as I am.

wings

{first published in February 2016}

There is something about growing, changing, identifying parts of yourself that you had not recognised, that is deeply unsettlingly liberating. I have been struggling to put words to it. Then today, a beautiful butterfly sat in my path. I remembered a poem by Dean Jackson that talks about a butterfly that was criticised by caterpillars for having changed, but the caterpillar like the changes because she now had wings!

Since I began to identify as Autistic no one has actually confronted me with disbelief that I could be. In fact the opposite has been true. People have welcomed me to the autistic community, told me they see it too, and encouraged me to continue looking at my life through this lens.

No one has called me weird, at least not to my face. No one has expressed their desire that I should be anything other than what I am comfortable being.

But there is an unsettling feeling there, in the core of my being, that this is how autistic people are seen by many in society, and that even though people who know me personally have been completely accepting of me, the people "out there" are not. I know it because I've seen it. I've seen the discrimination, aggression, and intolerance directed at my children and at my friends. I know one day I will face it too.

I know people will push back against my advocating for the rights of autistic people. My rights.

I know people will dismiss my advocacy as insignificant because they see their life as more important than the reality of autistic people. My reality.

I know people will stigmatise me the way I have seen them stigmatise the autistic community. My community.

I don't know how I will feel or respond when it happens. But I do know this: Rooting in my identity as an autistic person does not mean I am a different person. It does mean I am more complete, more full, and I am finding I am more capable of doing the things I want to when I acknowledge who I really am. It might look "weird" to others, but it is empowerment to me.

I have wings.

pathways

From my discussions with many autistic people, I've come to realise that for most of us it is part of a natural progression to go through a period of time when we "blame" everything on our autism.

You know, we have this new information and we are making sense of it. That involves looking at everything in your life through a new lens.

It is realising that misunderstanding that happened when you were 12 was entirely because you are autistic and the other people involved were not. You had a completely different experience than they did, because your sensory system and communication style is different than theirs, so of course there was a misunderstanding. It's a relief to realise that the situation wasn't because you are inadequate, a poor communicator, or lack social awareness. It was because you simply do things differently.

It is realising that the so called depression you've experienced, could well have been plain autistic burnout as a result of high intensity sensory experiences and some next level masking that became unsustainable. It's a relief to realise there is nothing wrong with your brain. It was just that your brain doesn't do things the way you thought it did. You just need to make some adjustments.

Along the pathways we walk to understanding ourselves better as late identified autistic adults, it makes perfect sense that we go through a period of time where everything seems like it could be because we are autistic.

And a lot of it is.

But some of it isn't.

Over time we realise that some of the struggles have been because someone else was being awful to us (not us doing something awful to them). Some of it was because someone misunderstood us (not we misunderstood them). We begin to realise that it wasn't all our fault. We are autistic, but we aren't always to blame.

It's reassuring to see research emerging now that recognises that the "blame" that has been put on autistic people for a lot of things …. lack of empathy, communication difficulties, awkward social situations …. can more realistically and fairly be attributed to differences between two people, not the differences in one person.

It's also wonderful to be seeing more and more research that explains why some of those differences exist. Evidence of neuronal differences. Identifying areas of our brains that are working differently than non autistic brains. Differently. Not broken.

These new pieces of information mean that we can know better what is happening and what we need.

It's fascinating to realise some of what I thought about myself previously was inaccurate! It's amazing to finally have an explanation that allows me to care for myself more effectively.

These pathways to understanding myself might look to others like inconsistencies, or like I was wrong before. It might look like I over reacted in the past, and I'm becoming more rational now. I would disagree.

I think the pathways of discovery we walk as we navigate the evolving understanding of our identities is a necessary and beautiful process that can be likened to walking a new bush trial and discovering something new and wonderful around every bend and corner.

human

Around another bend in my pathway to self understanding has been learning how complex all humans are. Similarly to realising that some of the challenges in our lives are because of other people, and not simply because we are autistic, at some point we also need to realise that even our internal struggles are not all caused by being autistic.

For a while all I could see was what my autism lens showed me. It was a necessary part of my progress along my pathway. But it wasn't always accurate, because it wasn't the whole story.

My studies in psychology, before I knew I was autistic, began to come back to me, and I have been reminded over the past few years of some things I have known for a long time, but needed to revisit to keep my self awareness more honest. We do lie to ourselves sometimes, don't we?

Particularly when the truth looks like creating hard work!

I am autistic, for sure.

I am also human.

Humans are complex creatures. We are made up of so many parts, ever changing. And we like familiar. All of us, not just the autistic ones! There are so many cognitive biases we use to process information, thoughts and feelings. Getting to the root of some of these has been essential in helping me see clearly the reasons why I do some of the things I do.

And not all of it is because I am autistic.

It is because I am human.

It is a normal part of the human experience to be tired. I may experience tiredness more frequently and intensely due to be autistic, but I get tired because I am human.

It is a normal part of the human experience to have emotional needs. The ways I get my emotional needs met, and the distress I experience when they aren't may be different than others because I am autistic, but I have emotional needs because I am human.

Do you see what I mean?

Learning about personality types, sensory systems, executive function quirks, communication styles and preferences, attachment theory, love languages, how trauma changes our brain, and much more has been incredibly helpful for me in creating strategies for living well.

If I had stopped at the discovery that I am autistic and assumed that was the reason for EVERYTHING I would have been missing out on so much of my own beautiful complexity!

mind

There are a few different theories about the Autistic mind. I'm not a researcher or a scientist, so I'm not going to try to explain them, and I'm not going to generalise about all Autistic peoples brains. My not research scientist reading, and my conversations with other people in the Autistic community, tells me that Autistic peoples minds are as complex and varied as those in any other group of people, and that there is nothing Autistic people experience that is outside of what is normal for human beings.

Something I notice about all people is that our minds, in their complexity, betray us. We think we can't do something, so we can't. We feel pain when we try, so our mind tells us to stop. It's why mind over matter is a saying, I suspect. For many the mind will give up before the body. I've experienced this with physical exercise. Some people give up out of boredom, some people give up when things are more challenging than expected.

As I have worked to understand myself better, I've wrestled with how much I can rely on my mind to give me accurate and helpful information. Do my thoughts always tell me the truth? I've learned to admit that they don't. I can misunderstand and misinterpret easily, as it turns out, and my mind must always be subject to double and triple checking.

Something I know to be true for myself, that is a stereotype applied to autistic people, is that I can be a very rigid thinker. Cognitive inflexibility plays a significant role in my every day, if I let it. Particularly so if I am very tired, or experiencing overwhelm. New evidence can present itself quite clearly and I will still maintain my viewpoint or resist changing my plan. It's not so much that I don't want to be flexible, but more that the energy it takes and the processing time required mean that it is incredibly difficult for me to pivot in the ways needed, and almost impossible for me to do so quickly. My mind tends toward "I can't" in those moments, and dragging it along for the flexibility is a monumental task. I have learned that "I'm going to need some time to think on that" is a supremely useful phrase.

Wisdom comes only from experience, and sometimes wisdom is doubting your own assumptions when it comes to your internal dialogues. There are few times this is more important than when I am anxious, scared or overwhelmed. In those moments, my thoughts will often betray me with disparaging self talk statements and over generalisations that only serve to limit me to preferring to stick with the familiar and predictable. Ironically, the mental gymnastics I do to keep myself aligned with the familiar and predictable is often more complex than the effort of adjusting to new. It still takes more energy to do the new, somehow, but I suppose that just shows how amazing our minds are at cognitive biases, and how careful we need to be to remain aware of them.

Complexity is complicated and messy and beautiful and necessary. And sometimes it causes us pain and work that we would be better off without. Sometimes we need to find the simplicity in life and to do that, for me at least, seems to involve challenging my own mind and thoughts.

body

Something that recent research has shown us is that autistic brains have more neuronal connections in them than non autistic brains. Though neurons are in our brains and spinal chords, they are linked to our nervous system through our whole body, which means this information helps us understand many things about the autistic body. The information our nerves send to our brains for processing goes through our neurons.

Very simplistically, this means that the autistic sensory experience of the world is more intense than the non-autistic sensory experience. We actually do feel more.

From anecdotal evidence- the stories people tell me and how similar they are to my experiences- I know that autistic people, though we don't all experience things exactly the same ways, can see brighter colours and notice more details, hear a greater range of frequencies and hear sounds more loudly, detect subtle smells, are very sensitive and reactive to taste and texture, and experience touch in a range of different ways that can both make it difficult to wear clothing at all and also make it difficult to notice body sensations. Sensory experience being atypical is a defining feature of autism.

Something I've noticed though, is that even though we experience the world more intensely, we seem to trust our bodies less. I can't help thinking that this is because we have been taught to ignore our bodies internal signals and messages about our experiences and what we need.

It happens so easily because our experiences aren't typical. When we say that something is too loud, and others don't find it too loud, we are told "no it's not". When we say something is overwhelming, and others don't find it overwhelming, we are told "don't be oversensitive- you'll be fine". It doesn't take too many times of that happening before we have learned that what our bodies tell us could be wrong and that other people can't be relied on to support or help us if we need it, so even if our bodies are right, there is no point saying anything.

The result of this is problematic at best, and quite dangerous at worst. Here's a personal example....

Every time I go to the supermarket or into a shopping mall I experience sensory overload to some degree. At its most extreme this experience leads to physical pain for me. These days I take measures to avoid this- sunglasses, headphones, choosing the day and time I go to avoid the busiest times, making sure I know exactly what I need and have a list written that has everything in the order I will find it in the shop so there is no time spent doubling back to get missed items. I shop in the same store whenever I can so I know where everything I need is. I rarely "window shop".

To an observer it would look like I am managing some pretty high level anxiety about shopping. In fact, for many years, I thought I was experiencing anxiety, and I didn't care for myself in the ways I do now. Then a couple of years ago I attended a brilliant workshop on anxiety, and what I heard helped me realise what the difference between fear and anxiety is. That workshop helped me to know that I wasn't anxious about shopping at all. I was experiencing fear. Fear of the predictable experience of pain.

The self care strategies required for fear and anxiety are quite different. So my lack of accurate reading of my body messages had lead to me misunderstanding myself and the result of that was inappropriate self care strategies.

As an adult I have options for education and growth and autonomy that aren't available to children. So autistic children are at risk of learning, as I did, to distrust their own bodies, and will learn to call their internal body cues by names that don't belong. Anxious instead of fearful. Oversensitive instead of hyperaware. Rude instead of assertive and self advocating. And it goes on.

It has taken me many years to begin to unlearn some of those words as applied to myself.

heart

"Heart" is an interesting concept, I think. Our heart is a literal organ that keeps us alive. And heart is a metaphor we use to refer to a variety of things, including our deepest feelings, our true (sometimes hidden) self, and to represent our emotions and feelings.

I use emotions and feelings to mean two different things, even though in much of our societal conversation the two words are interchangeable.

When I say emotions I am referring to the physiological process of neurotransmitters being secreted into our blood stream and creating an autonomic nervous system reaction that we interpret as being happiness, sadness, fear, disgust, anger, or surprise. Research shows that emotions are influenced by our limbic system and our sympathetic nervous system, so we don't have any control over them. In fact emotions happen subconsciously, and unless we learn to recognise them we often don't even realise we are having them!

When I say feelings I am talking about the conscious responses we have to our emotions when we assign meaning to them. Research shows that feelings originate in the neocortical region of the brain, including our frontal lobe, and that feelings are influenced by our thoughts. That is- we have some control over them. Because our feelings start with our emotions, it's pretty important that we do learn to recognise our emotions, otherwise we can end up having feelings we have created by thoughts about emotions we don't really understand, so the risk of our feelings being based on things that aren't helpful is pretty high!

When I talk about heart here, in this chapter of this book, I mean all the many nuanced and intricate emotions, feelings, thoughts, adaptive strategies, values and beliefs we hold that make us each into our own unique and wonderful selves.

And at the 'heart of the matter' when I talk about heart here, I am thinking on how our heart influences us to act in care of ourselves.

How do my emotions, feelings, thoughts, adaptive strategies, values and beliefs motivate me to care for my own individual needs?

Have I been hurt so much in the past that I don't trust anyone else to support me in meeting my needs?
Is my tendency toward independence helping me or holding me back from receiving the benefits of connection and community?
Have I had experiences that have fostered naivety in me that cause me to trust where I shouldn't?
Have I grown a belief that I am incompetent and incapable to the extent that I don't trust myself to meet my own needs and so I rely heavily on others?

I am wondering equally on how I, as an autistic person who experiences the world so intensely and who is predisposed to some extent toward a particular set of biases, can both guard my heart, and lovingly care for my heart, while existing in a world that doesn't understand me or try to help meet my needs.

Independence is essential.
Connection is essential.

The balancing of the two is a task unlike any other. And yet we must learn it if we are to live well-thriving and not merely surviving. I don't know two people whose balance looks the same. I don't know one person who has found a balance that can remain the same over long periods of time!

If I am being honest with myself, I have to admit that sometimes my heart is too defensive. I allow my thoughts to tell me stories that influence my feelings to be based on untruths. Sometimes it is because I had an awful experience in the past and I don't want to repeat it. Sometimes I'm just overgeneralising and being over protective.

Another honest admission is that there are times when my heart is too open. I pour it out into places that aren't safe and end up feeling hurt. I'll try to blame others for being careless with me, but truly I wasn't careful enough with myself.

Both these honest realisations are part of my experiences in life as someone whose sensory and emotional experiences of the world are intertwined and indescribably intense.

fierce

There is a song I listen to on repeat quite often. It's called "Steer" and it was written and recorded by Missy Higgins in 2008. The song opens with some of the most beautiful sensory imaging. But the part that really made me stop and listen the first time I heard the song was in the chorus when she sings, "…your heart is fierce, you finally know that you control where you go, you can steer".

That is the essence of the gift understanding myself as Autistic has been. Finally, I have a sense of being in control of things in my life, because I understand who I am and what I need. That's not to say that I now make the exact right decisions every time, or that I always anticipate my needs and make sure I don't push myself too hard, or extend myself too far, or that I don't make the mistake of not being adventurous enough, or that I never underestimate myself. But I am learning and getting it right more and more. The reality is that my needs are more often met and I am more confident, and living my life well.

We might think of fierce as an aggressive way of being. The definition of the word certainly conveys wildness, hostility, intensity and violence. I want to claim the word fierce as an appropriate way for an Autistic person to live. There are a few reasons for my use of the word fierce.

We link the idea of wildness with unpredictability and danger. I think that we suppress the instinct to be wild and adventurous, in favour of conformity and control. Fierce is an appropriate way to be when you are standing up against the expectation of submission and conformity.

We seem to find hostility highly offensive and something to be suppressed. I believe that hostility is is sign of unmet need, or even that rights have been unjustly ignored. The correct way to approach injustice and unmet needs, at a systemic level at least, is with ferocity, because never in human history have rights been defended with a meek and mild please and thank you.

We find intensity confronting and often seek to move away from it. When your experience of the world is entirely made up of intense and overwhelming experiences, intensely is the only way you know how to respond to things, and is a natural default for many people. Fierce is not wrong, any more than naturally intense is wrong, and it contributes to the beautiful diversity of humanity.

We link the concept of violence with being aggressive. I would argue that we too often confuse assertiveness with being aggressive, and that aggressive is a word too frequently used to silence assertive people. Silence can also be violent, particularly when silence is expected of people who are being oppressed. Fierce is an appropriate way to be when you are used to being silenced.

It is important to acknowledge the work done by Autistic people as we try to build a good life for ourselves. It is not easy to find who you really are when you are surrounded by constant messaging telling you what you should be, telling you what you should want to be. It is near impossible to feel authentic in yourself when the things you are told you should be are so completely different from who you know you are underneath the mask you wear in order to be accepted by others. It takes a lot of work, and a lot of courage.

The combination and balance of mind, body, and heart, and the work done to understand self and the interaction of these three is what helps us be brave- to do things even when we are scared and when we are overwhelmed- and that is what makes us fierce, a force to be reckoned with in a world that would rather we stay quiet and conform.

So I claim the ferocity that sits in me. I will recognise it with the intent of no longer forcing myself to be tame, meek, quiet and conforming. I will use my ferocity as empowerment to be wild when appropriate, hostile when necessary, unashamedly intense as my natural state, and noncompliant when I need to be.

My fierce heart is a part of me that is undeniably good, and I won't hide it.

www.ingramcontent.com/pod-product-compliance
Lightning Source LLC
Chambersburg PA
CBHW071840290426
44109CB00017B/1879